Don't Eat Soup with your Fingers

Compiled by John Foster

Illustrated by Agnese Baruzzi, Lee Cosgrove,
Clare Elsom, Andrés Martínez Ricci, Leo Broadley,
Yannick Robert, Sole Otero, Daron Parton,
Emi Ordás and Gemma Correll

Contents

Billie-Jean, The Ketchup Queen

Billie-Jean, Billie-Jean,
Billie-Jean, the Ketchup Queen.

She likes ketchup on her fries.
She likes ketchup on her pies.
She likes ketchup on her beans.
She likes ketchup on her greens.

She gets ketchup up her nose.
She gets ketchup on her toes.
She gets ketchup on her chair.
She gets ketchup on her hair.

Ketchup here. Ketchup there.
She gets ketchup everywhere.

Billie-Jean, Billie-Jean,
Covered in ketchup, the Ketchup Queen.

John Foster

Eggs with legs

Eggs with legs
Jumping from the pan,
Shouting to the cook,
'Catch us if you can!'

Pam Johnson

How did the egg get up the mountain?

It scrambled up.

What's the best thing to put in a pie?

Your teeth.

What has teeth but cannot eat?

A comb.

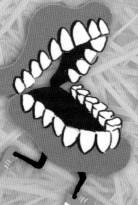

Why are false teeth like stars?

They come out at night.

Dinah's Diner

Don't stand there and be hungry.
Come in and be fed up.

When I Found a Large Mouse in my Stew

When I found a large mouse in my stew,
Said the waiter, 'Whatever you do,
Please do not shout
Or wave it about,
Or the rest will be wanting one, too!'

Anon

What is Worse?

What is worse than finding a worm
When you are eating a pear?
Taking a bite and then finding
There's half a worm left there!

Pam Johnson

Manners

Don't eat your soup with your fingers
It really isn't done.
Eat your fingers on their own.
Eat them one by one.

Kaye Umansky

Why did the boy throw away his doughnut?

Because it had a hole in it.

Name four things
that contain milk:

a milkshake,
a milk bottle
and two cows.

Batty Books

Cooking Made Easy by Mike Rowave

Quick Snack *by Roland Butter*

Side Salads by Tom Ato and Q. Cumber

Takeaway Meals by Donna Kebab

Sandwich Filler by P. Nutbutter

French Fries by Chris P. Crunchy

Sweet Treats by Candy Bar

The Boy Who Ate Too Much by Ivor Bellyache

The Cabbage is a Funny Veg.

The cabbage is a funny veg.
All crisp, and green, and brainy.
I sometimes wear one on my head
When it's cold and rainy.

Roger McGough

Why?

'Why are you wearing a cat as a hat?'
I asked my young friend Fred.
'Its fur keeps me warm on cold winter days
And a cow is too heavy,' he said.

Ian Ashendon

Animal Antics

Chimpanzees in dungarees
Play cards while picking off their fleas.

Kangaroos in high-heeled shoes
Sing and dance with cockatoos.

Alligators dressed as waiters
Play hide-and-seek with gladiators.

Elephants in stripy pants
Play basketball with giant ants.

But bumblebees on tiny skis
Struggle to juggle packs of peas.

Evie Lewis

The Hamster's Revenge

Nobody realized. Nobody knew.
The hamster was sleeping in my dad's shoe.

When he put it on, he trod on its nose.
So it opened its jaws and bit hard on his toes!

Paul Cookson

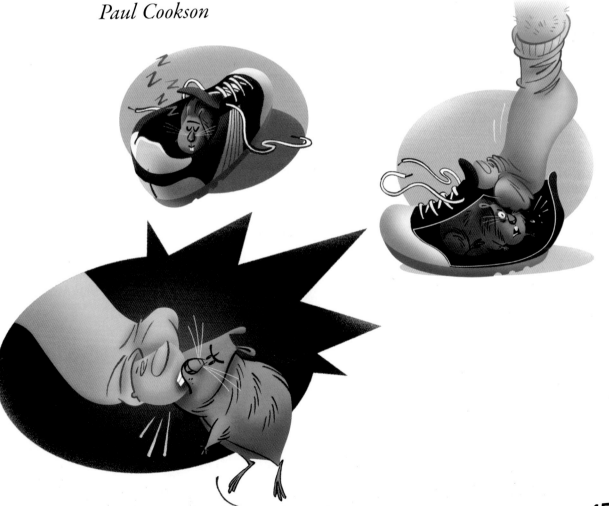

There Once was a Man from Bengal

There once was a man from Bengal
Who went to a fancy dress ball.
He said, 'I will risk it
And go as a biscuit,'
But a dog ate him up in the hall.

Anon

Fear

I'd rather be bitten by a snake
Or be melted alive by the sun.
I'd rather be eaten by spiders
Than be kissed in the playground by Mum.

Peter Dixon

Sorry it's Late

I haven't got my homework, Miss,
My sister stayed up late
But she couldn't do it all last night,
She said you'd have to wait.

She said the sums were harder
Than the ones you usually set
And that's the reason why
My homework isn't finished yet.

Derek Stuart

Why aren't We Paid for Going to School?

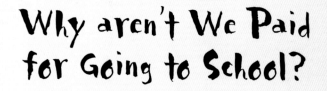

Why aren't we paid for going to school?
Don't you think it's funny
That we do all the hard work
But the teachers take the money!

John Foster

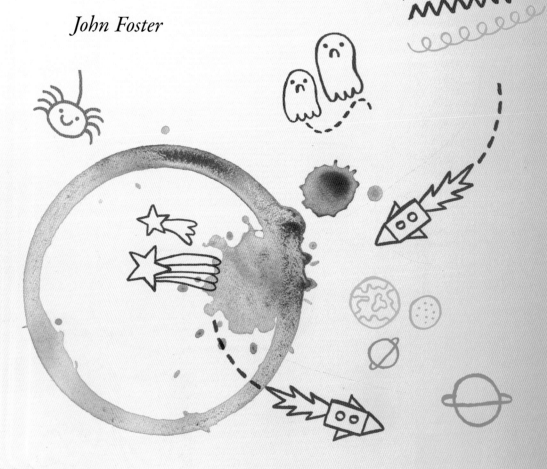

Please Let Me Stay at Home

Must I go to school?
Must I go today?
I'd rather stay at home
or go outside and play.

Must I see the teachers?
Can't I stay in bed?
School just isn't any fun
since they made me Head.

Andrew Collett

How did the dinner lady get an electric shock?

She stepped on a bun and a currant went up her leg.

About John Foster

I grew up in Carlisle and dreamed of
playing football for Carlisle United, but
they showed no interest in signing me. After working as
a firefighter in Canada, I became a teacher. That's when I
started to write poems and edit poetry books. I've written
about 1,500 poems and compiled over 100 anthologies.
But none of them have been as much fun as compiling the
Chucklers anthologies.

I've chuckled at the hamster getting revenge by biting
Dad's toes, giggled at the headteacher who doesn't want to
go to school, chortled at the batty books and laughed out
loud at the idea of wearing a cat as a hat rather than a cow.
Not to mention eating your fingers with your soup!